THE
BELLY OF THE
WHALE

Maureena Summers

THE
BELLY of the
WHALE

Maureena Summers

Unless otherwise indicated all scriptural quotations are taken from the King James Version of the Bible.

The Belly of the Whale
Copyright © 2018
Maureena Summers

Printed in the United States of America

Library of Congress – Catalogued in Publication Data

ISBN: 9781729364765
Imprint: Independently published

Publishing and Editorial Assistance:
Jabez Books Writers' Agency
(A Division of Clark's Consultant Group)
www.clarksconsultantgroup.com
wwwJabezbooks.com

Cover designed by James Nesbit

Foreword

By Apostle Pam Vinette

The world went dark; the room spun out of control. It felt like nothing would ever be the same again. A silent hush went out that seemed eternal. She had gotten that message before, "Mrs. Summers, your son Kelvin has been shot." But this time, it was followed by the words no mother should ever have to hear, "I'm so sorry for your loss." Your loss, not your best friend's loss, your first Sunday School teacher's loss, your loss. The words seemed so hollow, as if those who spoke them went to some dreadful simpering school of humanistic mercy from which they could not graduate until they proved how glibly they could espouse them.

For Maureena Heard Summers, her children were her life. Although she had the first two under unfavorable circumstances, her love for them was unquestionable. Abusive, abandoning relationships with their fathers, youthful vanity left her alone with her darling boys literally a child raising children. Thank God for family, for they were her "soft place" to land as she searched for something to get her through the overwhelming responsibilities of being a single mom.

Single moms often do the best that they can in every circumstance but when they are in the world, the world finds a way to creep inside of them and capture their soul. Whenever this happens the truth of "fun in sin for a season" suddenly brings them to the reality of hell's incessant quest for the souls of all men, and it seems to them, especially their children before salvation.

An unfortunate accident scarred her baby boy, Kelvin, for life, which began a domino effect of overcompensating for the failure to protect him. Drowning in an alternate lifestyle of drugs and debauchery, Maureena turned her eyes toward heaven and found a peace she never dreamt possible.

This decision enabled her to breath in the fatal, horrific night of her son's demise. That dark night was not the first dark night experience by this prophetess. The most formidable nights were yet ahead, and she would have been utterly undone were it not for her rock, her Savior and Lord, Jesus Christ and her precious husband, Rick, who shared her Christ and her grief, and a crowd of spiritual and natural family members who loved hard and would not let go of her. Oh, we say we trust God and admonish others to do so all the time when we are Christians, but what do we say to a mother who must face burying her baby when she's ridden with guilt and pain? It seems that the words have not been created until we find that space in time to remember to place ourselves in her space before we answer. That is what it means to enter into "The Belly of the Whale."

Maureena knows the hateful pain of losing someone she loves to the brutality of murder.

You are numb; all the air is sucked out of the room as you try to process in a dreamlike state how to get up on your feet to awaken from the all-encompassing nightmare. But in the middle of the disbelieve and extreme sorrow, God showed up for me, and she watched Him show up for her. She can't lie and say it happened overnight, but she can say it happened!

Immediately, she felt the huge, able arms of the Lord swept into the uncontrollable fear, anger and grief that were present in the room. A strange peace overwhelmed her as she gave herself permission to rise above the circumstances and experience blessed memories and happy moments with the one she loved now more than ever.

This book is an anthology of this prophet's journey to peace and triumph. This prophet is more alive now than ever and her adored Kelvin lives and shines brightly through her obedient life. Light has pierced the darkness and this book has become the catharsis that we each need in our own lives to replace the things that go "bump in the dark nights" of life. Jesus is her constant, and it is her desire that you come to know Him through her transparency.

As you read this exemplary exposé of God's grace, favor and overwhelming love, read it from the standpoint of it being a judge in your life. Allow it to be a judge in all aspects of your life. Whether it is your failures or successes, allow it to reveal that which is not readily identifiable to you. But especially judge your own failures against her revelation of God's ability to triumph through them, along with deciding to overcome them, forgive them, to rise high above them.

Be sure to grab a cup of hot coco, a soft blanket, a big box of tissues and a secluded spot in which to laugh, cry and praise your most excellent God for His most delightful gift of love. Don't forget to pray for Prophetess Maureena, her husband, Wallice, sons: Kevin and Emery; Daughters: Jazz and Shalethia; Grandchildren: Airiana, Ahona, Saynia, Serenity, Kvion, Nihim, Kennedy, Terrence, TeTa; Great-Grandchildren: Taylen and Duka; and my dear Michelle (daughter in Law) with April and Rico. When sin steals in death it ravages a whole family until prayer and Jesus brings peace to each private storm.

Let the stories in this book fill your life with the light of His love as you walk the steps with Maureena, as she and her family are lovingly escorted by the Lord out of "The Belly of the Whale."

CONTENTS

THE CRY
OF A HEART

Jonah 1

The LORD gave this message to Jonah son of Amittai: "Get up and go to the great city of Nineveh. Announce my judgment against it because I have seen how wicked its people are."

But Jonah got up and went in the opposite direction to get away from the LORD. He went down to the port of Joppa, where he found a ship leaving for Tarshish. He bought a ticket and went on board, hoping to escape from the LORD by sailing to Tarshish.

But the LORD hurled a powerful wind over the sea, causing a violent storm that threatened to break the ship apart. Fearing for their lives, the desperate sailors shouted to their gods for help and threw the cargo overboard to lighten the ship.

But all this time Jonah was sound asleep down in the hold. So the captain went down after him. "How can you

sleep at a time like this?" he shouted.
"Get up and pray to your god! Maybe
he will pay attention to us and spare
our lives."

The crew cast lots to see which of them
had offended the gods and caused the
terrible storm. When they did this, the
lots identified Jonah as the
culprit. "Why has this awful storm
come down on us?" they demanded.
"Who are you? What is your line of
work? What country are you from?
What is your nationality?"

Jonah answered, "I am a Hebrew, and
I worship the LORD, the God of heaven,
who made the sea and the land."

The sailors were terrified when they heard this, for he had already told them he was running away from the LORD. "Oh, why did you do it?" they groaned. And since the storm was getting worse all the time, they asked him, "What should we do to you to stop this storm?"

"Throw me into the sea," Jonah said, "and it will become calm again. I know that this terrible storm is all my fault."

Instead, the sailors rowed even harder to get the ship to the land. But the stormy sea was too violent for them, and they couldn't make it. Then they cried out to the LORD, Jonah's God. "O LORD," they pleaded, "don't make us *die for this man's sin. And don't hold us responsible for his death. O LORD, you have sent this storm upon him for your own good reasons."*

Then the sailors picked Jonah up and threw him into the raging sea, and the storm stopped at once! The sailors were awestruck by the LORD's great power, and they offered him a sacrifice and vowed to serve him.

Now the LORD had arranged for a great fish to swallow Jonah. And Jonah was inside the fish for three days and three nights.

Jonah in the Bible is an Old Testament prophet who tried to run from God by boarding a ship to a city opposite of the one God was calling him to go to. In his desire to flee God's desire for his life, Jonah ended up in the belly of a whale. While in the belly of the whale, Jonah had time to reflect on the choices he made, the decisions other people had made, and how these decisions had affected him. So after much reflection in the belly of the whale, Jonah prayed. Jonah cried out to God and God heard him, delivered him, and set him free from the belly of the whale.

This book is about my journey with my son Kelvin, who was shot and killed in the back of his head, in what is called a cold-blooded murder.

When a mother loses a child, there is a pain that is unexplainable, and unless you have lost a child, you cannot even begin to comprehend the amount of grief that can be felt. However, while in the belly of the whale, which was a place for me to process the loss of my son, the Lord visited me and I was able to reflect on the life of my son, my choices, his choices, and how those choices affected other people. I cannot bring my son back from the dead, but I can share the story of his life through my eyes and how God has healed my heart through this process.

I have been in grief counseling for over a year now, and honestly, I waited way too long to go into counseling, thinking I could overcome this tragedy on my own, but I saw things in my own life that were cries of a soul that was still hurting for the loss of a son. So, after a year of grief counseling, my counselor suggested that I write a book to document my journey of his life, which was so interconnected with my life.

This book is the result of this process. My prayer is that my grief, my memories, and my story will be a reminder to you, that there is hope on the other side of the belly of the whale. And that there is a God in heaven who hears the cry of your heart, while you are in the belly of the whale, and that you realize you are not alone.

I invite you to join me on this journey as I share with you the celebrations, challenges, and choices that are called life which brought me into the belly of the whale and also got me out of it. I will never forget my son, but I can't live at his grave. If I want him to have a legacy and

I want to live the abundant life, I had to remove the grave clothes off of my mind. Death is painful, and yes, the death of a child is a most painful experience, but I know the resurrection and the life giver – Jesus Christ. It was He alone that delivered me out of the belly of the whale.

I hope you stay for this whole journey; it was a rough start, but even in death, God had a way of turning darkness into light, death into life, and mourning into dancing.

Kelvin died April 5, 2011 and so did I. But now, I am learning to live again. Only Jesus can do this. Only Jesus can heal the pain to the place where I can live again without feeling guilty for living. Only Jesus can restore my life and make a ministry out of my tragedy. There is no one else that could heal my heart; for no one else could understand my pain. Remember, our Father which art in heaven, lost His son in a tragic death as well, but His death was for our life, so He more than anyone else can understand the pain we feel at the loss of our children. I know now, from personal experience, that He truly is the God of all compassion, who brings life from death.

I would be honored for you to take this journey with me as I share my healing process by telling you about my boy, Kelvin. Come with me inside the belly of the whale.

Jonah 2

Then Jonah prayed to the LORD his God from

inside the fish. He said,

"I cried out to the LORD in my great trouble,

and he answered me.

I called to you from the land of the dead,[b]

and LORD, you heard me!

You threw me into the ocean depths,

and I sank down to the heart of the sea.

The mighty waters engulfed me;

I was buried beneath your wild and stormy

waves.

Then I said, 'O LORD, you have driven me from

your presence.

Yet I will look once more toward your holy

Temple.'

"I sank beneath the waves,

and the waters closed over me.

Seaweed wrapped itself around my head.

I sank down to the very roots of the

mountains.

I was imprisoned in the earth,

whose gates lock shut forever.

But you, O LORD my God,

snatched me from the jaws of death!

As my life was slipping away,

I remembered the LORD.

And my earnest prayer went out to you

in your holy Temple.

Those who worship false gods

turn their backs on all God's mercies.

But I will offer sacrifices to you with songs of

praise, and I will fulfill all my vows.

For my salvation comes from the LORD alone."

Then the LORD ordered the fish to spit Jonah

out onto the beach.

Chapter 1

THE EARLY YEARS

Psalm 139:1-14

¹*O LORD, you have examined my heart*

and know everything about me.

² *You know when I sit down or stand up.*

You know my thoughts even when I'm far

away.

³ *You see me when I travel*

and when I rest at home.

You know everything I do.

⁴ *You know what I am going to say*

even before I say it, LORD.

⁵ *You go before me and follow me.*

You place your hand of blessing on my head.

⁶ *Such knowledge is too wonderful for me,*

too great for me to understand!

7 I can never escape from your Spirit!

I can never get away from your presence!

8 If I go up to heaven, you are there;

if I go down to the grave,[a] you are there.

9 If I ride the wings of the morning,

if I dwell by the farthest oceans,

10 even there your hand will guide me,

and your strength will support me.

11 I could ask the darkness to hide me

and the light around me to become night—

12 but even in darkness I cannot hide from you.

To you the night shines as bright as day.

Darkness and light are the same to you.

13 You made all the delicate, inner parts of my

body and knit me together in my mother's

womb.

14 Thank you for making me so wonderfully

complex!

Your workmanship is marvelous—how well

I know it.

15 You watched me as I was being formed in

utter seclusion, as I was woven together in

the dark of the womb.

16 You saw me before I was born.

Every day of my life was recorded in your

book. Every moment was laid out

before a single day had passed.

17 How precious are your thoughts about

me, O God.

They cannot be numbered!

18 I can't even count them; they outnumber the

grains of sand! And when I wake up,

you are still with me!

Do you remember the day you found out you were pregnant? For some, it was a surprise, for others it was planned, but either way, the announcement that you were carrying another human being in your body was possibly the most exhilarating feeling in the world – a dream come true. But in the midst of this joy and happiness, there can also be fear, uncertainty, and worry. I experienced all of this. Much of this anxiety was because I was not married, actually I was only 17 years old. My boyfriend Kevin and I were both young, naïve and immature, but here we were about to have a baby, a baby boy. The thoughts, the dreams, the ideas I had about what he was going to be when he grew up flooded my mind as I thought about this little person inside of me. But, in the same breath, I was nervous, for I was still a child in many respects.

Kevin and I were not married, nor did we plan on getting married, our relationship had some significant challenges even before this situation. Kevin was verbally and physically abusive toward me, and being young and in love, I overlooked those faults in him, but now I was pregnant, and it was not just about me. I had another person to think about. It took me a while to make the much-needed break from him, but the birth of this child was definitely going to change things for us and we both knew this, even though we did not act on it immediately. Challenges, honestly, led us to end our relationship shortly after the birth of our son.

We were living in Des Moines, IA when on November 23, 1985 we gave birth to our son Kelvin Lee Heard. He came into the world weighing 7 pounds, 0 ounces. We were so enamored by this little man that was placed into our arms that day. Just like all parents, we thought he was perfect. Those little fingers and toes all in perfect union, those feet that I could not resist kissing, that face, oh that face. There is truly nothing like looking into the face of something God allowed you to help create. I had to kiss his face as soon as I saw it, he was the essence of purity, truly a gift from heaven.

Shortly after Kelvin's birth, I had to make one of the hardest decisions of my life -- to leave Kelvin's dad. I had to. It was for our safety. Unfortunately, Kevin was physically abusive to me and I could not take it anymore. So, right now, I was not only concerned about myself, but also about this little man that was in my care. The physical abuse and consistent infidelity, by Kevin, finally pushed me to edge of my tolerance level, so I decided enough is enough.

In addition to my personal issues with Kelvin's father, it was discovered that Kelvin (the baby) had some physical challenges as well. He was allergic to milk. We had to raise him on soy products, so he could get the nutrients he needed to thrive as a baby. To say we had many challenges as a family is an understatement.

Being a new mom, having to deal with an abusive and cheating boyfriend, and now a child who had a milk allergy, was a lot for me as a young mom.

I was not mature enough to handle all of these things coming at me at once. Now years later, as I reflect, it seems so minor, but then it felt so major and I just did not know how to be a girlfriend and mother of two. You see, I had another son from another man, so Kelvin was not my first son, he was actually my second. So here I was a kid, trying to raise kids, and in many ways on my own as Kevin was an absent father from the start. Not absent physically as he was home now and then, but absent emotionally as he was with other women and spiritually as he was living for himself and no one else. I was tired, scared and honestly, did not make these kids a priority, so I asked for help from family

Now, I am a single mom, just freshly turned 18 years old and my son is not yet 1 years old. Thinking now we are out of that abusive situation, so things are about to turn around for us, but actually, it got worse before it got better.

as it pertained to taking care of them, until I could figure out how to do it on my own.

For me to get out of this abusive relationship, I had to go into hiding for six months, so Kelvin's father could not find Kelvin and me. This hiding led us to eventually move to Minnesota where I had family I could stay with as we transitioned into a life apart from Kelvin. Now, I am a single mom, just freshly turned 18 years old and my son is not yet one year old. Thinking now we are out of that abusive situation, so things are about to turn around for us, but actually, it got worse before it got better. I was struggling with the pain of the abuse, the responsibilities of raising two children and those pressures caused me to make poor choices. To deal with the stress of the situation

I was in and the pain of the abusive relationship, I turned to alcohol and drug use, which hindered my ability to make responsible choices for my little family.

I was working, but I was also doing drugs with friends, which meant I had to leave Kelvin with family members to watch him. Little did I realize those choices would have lasting ramifications on me as a mom and on my son, Kelvin.

Now without a father in the house, Kelvin was being taken care of by family members and while I was at work one day, a family member put Kelvin in a bath tub that was so hot it burned him to the point of having scars on his legs that lasted his whole life. This event was traumatic for both Kelvin and myself as I am experiencing mom guilt even know as I remember that incident of which I was not there to protect my son. Kelvin was only one year old when this bathtub incident happened, and this combined with my poor choices with drugs, led to the removal of my son from me as a mother. Kelvin was put into foster care for eight months because of my immature behavior and choices. While Kelvin was in foster care, because I could not take care of my own son, I had to face some hard realities. I was dealing with mom guilt, the pain of an abusive relationship, my own selfish behavior with drug use and alcohol and the stress of being a single mom. I had family around me and without their love and support, I may not have made it through this very dark time in my life.

Kelvin's legs being burned, impacted me more significantly than I realized, for the scars on his legs lasted throughout his childhood and he was picked on for having scars on his legs and I knew it was because of my negligence and the pain of this reality was at times too hard to bear.

The amount of guilt I felt, and honestly even as I write this, I am still feeling the pain, as I reflect on this incident is tremendous. Not knowing how to process the burns on my son's legs, the negligent behavior I engaged in, the abuse from his father and all the other issues that were happening at that time, led to me to over compensate when it came to Kelvin. I decided when he was taken away, that when he comes back to me, I will make him my priority and I will give him anything he wants, little did I know, this would be another level of trouble for him.

I honestly thought I could appease my guilt, by being whatever he needed whenever he needed it. I had fallen in the ditch of neglect as it pertained to my son, he had the scars to prove it, literally, so unbeknownst to me, I jumped into the other ditch of trying to be all things to him. I made him my world, my life, my passion, I did everything for that boy in a way to try to appease the guilt I was feeling for neglecting him.

I worked in order to make sure he always had the latest and greatest of everything. No one was going to call my son neglected, because I was going to prove he wasn't by my spoiling him: I was not a bad mom and that he was not neglected. So, needless to say, I gave him everything he wanted, not knowing that I went from the ditch of neglect to the other ditch of indulgence and neither ditch was going to bring my son life, but both would eventually lead to his death.

Kelvin's childhood normalized for the most part. I got a job, working to provide for the family and where I was unable to support, we had family who helped in those areas. During these years we managed to live a normal life for people who did not know Jesus, but who loved one another.

Kevin, (the dad) of course, was not "in the picture," so two boys growing up without a dad, had its own challenges we had to deal with, but it made me stronger as a mom. I was able to set boundaries that the boys needed in order to thrive in life. They went to school and did well throughout their elementary years, but as they got into the preteen and teenage years, we began to see the manifestation of some behaviors that would produce some lifestyles that proved detrimental.

I had to work, they had no dad and despite our best efforts as a family, there were somethings we could not control, one being the influence of peers on my boys' lives and the anger they had because of not having a dad in the house. I did all I could as a mom, but raising boys means they need that male figure in their lives to show them how to be a man, how to say no to some things and how to navigate the waters or puberty, peer pressure and various other problems. So, since I was not a man, I could not help them with some of these challenges. With this said, so they turned to their friends and we all know that peers are not equipped to help young men become real men. This was truly another challenge for me and a new season.

Chapter 2

CHALLENGES AND CHOICES

Joshua 24:14-24

"So fear the LORD and serve him wholeheartedly. Put away forever the idols your ancestors worshiped when they lived beyond the Euphrates River and in Egypt. Serve the LORD alone. But if you refuse to serve the LORD, then choose today whom you will serve. Would you prefer the gods your ancestors served beyond the Euphrates? Or will it be the gods of the Amorites in whose land you now live? But as for me and my family, we will serve the LORD."

The people replied, "We would never abandon the LORD and serve other gods. For the LORD our God is the one who rescued us and our ancestors from slavery in the land of Egypt. He performed mighty miracles before our very eyes. As we traveled through the wilderness among our enemies, he preserved us. It was the LORD who drove out the Amorites and the other nations living here in the land. So we, too, will serve the LORD, for he alone is our God."

Then Joshua warned the people, "You are not able to serve the LORD, for he is a holy and jealous God. He will not forgive your rebellion and your sins.

If you abandon the LORD and serve other gods, he will turn against you and destroy you, even though he has been so good to you."

But the people answered Joshua, "No, we will serve the LORD!"

"You are a witness to your own decision," Joshua said. "You have chosen to serve the LORD."

"Yes," they replied, "we are witnesses to what we have said."

"All right then," Joshua said, "destroy the idols among you, and turn your hearts to the LORD, the God of Israel."

The people said to Joshua, "We will serve the LORD our God. We will obey him alone."

L ife is a journey of discovery. Therefore, I believe we are created to discover different aspects of life from childhood to adulthood and every other "hood" in between. Living in Minneapolis, Des Moines, and eventually Tulsa, OK, my family and I knew what life was like in our little hoods. It was not Compton in South Los Angeles or the Southside of Chicago, nor was it the Bronx in New York, but it was a neighborhood with people who were facing challenges and making poor choices.

Many of the boys in our neighborhood grew up in single parent homes. The moms were doing the best they could, just like I was to raise boys in a world where there was an absence of fathers, but we did the best we could. Unfortunately, when these boys became teenagers, they started to get a mind of their own and many of us moms thought they were losing their minds, because we forgot we acted in many ways just like them, but our parents seemed to be so much more strict and we didn't like that, so maybe, if I'm honest, I loosened the grip at a time when I should have tightened it.

As I mentioned early, driven by mom guilt, I resorted to giving Kelvin anything he wanted. So when the high tops called Jordan's came out, I made sure my son had a pair, when he needed or wanted new clothes, I got it for him. I always made sure my boy was on the cutting edge of that which was popular. But, along with being spoiled by his mom, no dad in his life and now being in junior high school, Kelvin not only had the influence of his older brother, who was not making good choices, he had the pressure of his friends to join them in some behaviors that were detrimental to him.

Being the younger brother, he looked up to his older brother and wanted to do whatever he and his friends were doing. His older brother's influence on Kelvin was profound, for in many ways, his older brother was the only male role model he knew, and his older brother was trying to find his way, despite being followed by his younger brother. So, as brothers, they did everything together, which offered Kelvin the ability to do things his older brother and their friends were doing, despite his age being younger.

Kelvin and his older brother, along with all their friends were trying to navigate a man's world without a man in their life. There is an old saying that says, if a blind man leads a blind man, both of them will fall in a ditch, Unfortunately, this saying was true for my boys, as they were like the blind leading the blind. Despite the challenges and poor choices my sons were making, there was a ray of hope beginning to shine in our lives. Though it did

> *Despite the challenges and poor choices my sons were making, there was a ray of hope beginning to shine in our lives.*

not take root on a level I would have liked early on, my choice to follow Jesus, was the hope that was going to start to help our family. I realized that my boys were a reflection of me, since I was raising them and it was time for me to surrender my life to Christ, for I needed help and the pain was so deep from the abusive relationship, the traumatic incident with Kelvin in the bathtub and my own personal choices, that when I gave my life to Christ, I was all in.

I made those boys come to church with me, I began to sing on the worship team, I stayed single and devoted my life to Jesus only and my family. Light was shining in the darkness of my life and that light would be the very thing that saved our families life, or all of us could have ended up dead.

As much as I would like to think this book is a story about Kelvin, of which it is, it is actually a book about the saving power of Jesus Christ and it started when I surrendered my life to Him as my personal Lord and Savior. I knew I could not give something to my sons that I did not have for myself, but I also quickly learned, I could model this new life, I could require attendance at church, but I could not change their hearts, despite my greatest efforts, so I had to lean on the everlasting arms, learn to pray, engage in spiritual warfare and wrestle the enemy in the belly of the whale in order to be transformed into a woman after God's own heart. I could only model this new life for my sons, I could not legislate it in their lives. They would eventually have to make their own decisions about this man Jesus and His power to change our lives, He did it for me and I knew He could do it for them, but I had to pray and be patient as I waited for God to work on the hearts of my sons.

Many times, when we surrender to Jesus, things seem to go from bad to worse, before they get better. This was the case in our lives. Kelvin is in junior high school and his grades are dropping drastically. I come to find out the reason is because he is not even in school. He was skipping school along with his brother and their friends. I was working full time, so I assumed that they were going to school when they got up in the morning and headed that way, but that was not the case and their grades were evidence

What I did not change was my giving things to Kelvin...Looking back I realize I was blessing his disobedience...so he continued to make poor choices.

not boys that were stupid, but of boys that were engaged in behaviors that were contrary to a learning environment. Kelvin was skipping school, so his grades reflected his lack of attendance and this drove him deeper into friendships that were problematic, not out of them.

Being a single mom, I could not quit my job, but I did address the issue of attendance, the importance of education and the need for personal responsibility, in addition to going even harder on Kelvin's older brother, knowing that Kelvin was following his lead.

What I did not change was my giving things to Kelvin, despite the poor behavior choices. Looking back I realize I was blessing his disobedience and so without him having to experience those consequences for his choices, he continued to make poor choices. It has been said that hindsight is 20/20 and I see that to be true today, as I reflect on how much I gave them despite how irresponsible they were acting. I knew they were not making the right decisions, but I felt bad that they did not have a dad and was glad that they were doing the best they could, so I saw the gifts as ways of encouraging them rather than spoiling them. Little did I know that these decisions on my part were actually perpetuating a behavior pattern that was destructive for my sons rather than constructive. I never taught them to curb their appetite, by teaching them to say no for I could not say no to them when they wanted something.

I think we as parents do the best we can in the situation we are in, then when we look back we realize where we made our mistakes. If you have made mistakes in the way you raised your children, know you are not alone. Hindsight is 20/20, but if you had 20/20 vision in the present situation you would have made a different decision. It is easy to beat ourselves up for the wrong decisions we made while parenting our children, but thanks be to God who has forgiven us for all our sins, including those we made while raising our children. God is the only perfect parent, the rest of us are learning to be parents while on the job. There is grace for the race. I had to learn this and this book is part of that process of restoration for the enemy loves to beat us up for everything we did wrong, because he is a master of the past, but God is the Father of the future and an ever-present help in time of trouble, so we lean on Him, we let him say who we are, not our past.

I did make some great choices with my boys as well as some mistakes. I taught them to have a good work ethic. Kelvin had a dog walking business when he was 13 years old, being an entrepreneur myself, it was important for me to instill in these boys a work ethic that would sustain them in the years to come. So, along with the seeds of pain and destruction, we were able to sow seeds of hope, life and production, so they sensed that there was more to them than their current situation of skipping school, hanging with their friends and making poor choices.

Looking back, I remember that Kelvin and his brother were left home alone a lot, as I had to work to provide for our family. This independence was to prove detrimental to them as they got involved in partying, drugs, alcohol and girls, which for most teenagers is typical behavior, but with no parental figure on site, due to dad being absent and mom working, their family became their friends and so they did what their friends did. I will say this, though, on more than one occasion I would find them at a party and literally drag their butts out of that situation, for this behavior was not acceptable to me.

Throughout all of their junior high and high school days, we battled with the peer pressure and school attendance. The desire to fit in with friends and party was more important to them than getting good grades, so I had to shift focus when Kelvin got a little older, for traditional school was not working for him.

Kelvin joined the job corps, which is like vocational training or on the job training, where he could obtain a skill that will prepare him for a job. Traditional school was not working for him, so we transferred him into this program, but he was so deeply rooted in his peer influences that he ended up dropping out of school and job corps and just hanging with his friends all day long. Drugs and alcohol were the norm for them and it was providing a source of income, so now he is feeling like he has something going. The challenge was, despite my best efforts to share from personal experiences that this was not a beneficial route to take, he chose this route, and little did either of us know it would lead to him having an early end to his life.

For me, personally, I was praying, prophesying and decreeing the salvation of my sons, like never before. I continued in the worship ministry at my church and actually really enjoyed not only singing but hearing the voice of God and using what I heard in prayer, to eventually move into the prophetic. True intercessors that can hear the voice of God are where true prophets and prophetesses are born and my desire to pray, to intercede and to prophesy came out of praying for my boys and worship. So, while they were making poor choices of which I could manage, but not control, I was drawing near to the Lord in a way I had not known was possible before. My heart was healing, my calling was being solidified and dreams were coming alive inside of me. Not apart from my boys, but for them and with them. I saw them saved and serving God with me, I still do!

After dropping out of job corps, Kelvin got his GED, for having some form of education was important to me, for I value education and I wanted my sons to value it as well. I believed and still believe that education instills values that we need to be a success in many areas of life. After he got his GED, he found a carpentry school that he really enjoyed, and he picked up the trade of carpentry, but the drinking and drugs did not cease, they actually began to increase for he was getting older and more street wise. In 2001 for a variety of reasons, we moved to Tulsa, Oklahoma, one of them being I wanted to put Kelvin in a new city, with the hopes of him changing some of his behaviors, since he was now a trained carpenter. Obtaining a new environment was part of my desire toward his deliverance from drugs and alcohol, but just like water seeks its level, so my son sought out people that would do drugs with him and go drinking with him. So, even though we were in a new city, I still had the same son.

Tulsa proved to enhance not decrease the illegal activity Kelvin got himself into to support his drinking and drug habit. He was stealing cars as one of his part- time jobs and his brother had just been sentenced to jail in Minnesota for drug possession charges. So, with the news of Kelvin's older brother and his new level of stealing, drinking and drugs, Kelvin got himself thrown in jail.

> *I was devastated, both my boys were in jail and for me Tulsa, God told me was my promised land, but the giants in that land got my son and into jail he went.*

I was devastated, both my boys were in jail and for me Tulsa, God told me was my promised land, but the giants in that land got my son and into jail he went. So, with one son in jail in

Minnesota and one in jail in Tulsa, all I could do was draw near to the Lord in prayer, fasting and Bible reading, speaking into their lives through prayer, prophesying over their lives and asking God to intervene in their lives. Before going to jail Kelvin had become a daddy and his girlfriend gave birth to a baby girl. This little lady stole my son's heart, but not enough to get him to change his behavior. His daughters name is Arianna and she is my granddaughter who still lives in Tulsa.

Now with Kelvin in jail, his daughter being raised by a single mom, who herself in many ways is still a child and no support from Kelvin, the generational cycle was growing and I was praying, binding, loosing, decreeing and declaring, seeking to influence my son, but the choices were still his to make. If we don't understand that prayer has the power to persuade but cannot control an outcome we can get disappointed if our prayers are not answered the way we are praying them. Many people get mad at God for not saving their children the way they think they should be saved, or healing their body in their time, or whatever the issue may be, and honestly, I struggled with those exact thoughts. However, I have learned the hard way that God does not control anyone, our prayers influence people, but the choice still lies with the person. This is a hard reality to accept, but it is the truth and once we accept this as truth we will cease to be mad at God for the people we love's inability to say yes to such a merciful and kind King.

Kelvin is in jail for drug possession and auto theft, his daughter is here in Tulsa, and I am in what I believe is my promised land. I get involved heavily in the church here, called Transformation Church and I meet a woman that is to become my mentor named Prophetess Brenda. She was truly a rock in the storms that I went through there in Tulsa, but she also taught me to pray, and she helped me to mature. She took me under her wing as a daughter and trained me in the ways of intercession, prophesy and prayer, like I had not known prior. God was setting me up for the season I was about to enter, but I did not know it at the time. Kelvin was living with a lot of personal pain, anger and unhealed emotions from his childhood of not having a dad around, but he chose drugs, alcohol and the street lifestyle to deal with the pain and that unwillingness to deal with the pain, drove him deeper into drugs and alcohol. All in all, he spent six years in and out of prison with felonies for a variety of charges.

We serve a merciful God, he does not allow us to reap the full consequences of our choices, but there are laws that must be followed on earth in order to maintain justice, peace and order in our streets. Tulsa police made sure Kelvin reaped the consequences of his choices with drugs and car theft, this is what kept him in prison while living in the city I was hoping this city would be a transformation place for him, like it was for me. Little did I know, it would be the last city he would ever know.

Kelvin was in and out of jail multiple times and while in jail on one of his sentences, his best friend was murdered in prison. This experience was traumatic for Kelvin, even though he did not verbalize how much it affected him, his behavior after this incident descended into increased moral decay, drugs and alcohol. Now, my little boy is a man and I am losing more and more control of what he does, not because I don't love him, but because he is unable to receive my love anymore due to the intense pain that has riddled him his whole life. Now to add insult to injury, his best friend dies, and the grief turned to anger, and the anger is expressed in drugs, alcohol and running with a harder group of guys than he had run with previously.

I could sense in my spirit my son was in danger, so I prayed for his protection; tried to speak to him about his choices, but I knew I could not make him behave, despite the warnings I felt in my spirit that he was approaching his end if he did not make some major changes.

As parents we can do our best in raising our children, we can hang on with all our heart to the Word of God that promises us if we train a child in the way they should go, they will never depart from it, but just like Jonah did not agree with God's direction for his life and ended up in the belly of a whale, sometimes despite our best efforts, our children make choice that put them in the belly of that same whale. One of the hardest things for me as a mother was to watch my son, engage in behaviors that I could not make him stop engaging in; to live with a pain that I could not heal him of; and run with a crowd that I could not stop him from running with. In our moments of feeling so helpless, we may try to control, manipulate or even coerce our children into doing the right thing, for in our eyes, that will always be my baby, but despite my best efforts, there was nothing I could do, He made his choice and I had to pray that mercy would triumph over judgment.

Chapter 3

DEATH OF A DREAM

Ezekiel 37:1-14

The LORD took hold of me, and I was carried away by the Spirit of the LORD to a valley filled with bones. He led me all around among the bones that covered the valley floor. They were scattered everywhere across the ground and were completely dried out. Then he asked me, "Son of man, can these bones become living people again?"

"O Sovereign LORD," I replied, "you alone know the answer to that."

Then he said to me, "Speak a prophetic message to these bones and say, 'Dry bones, listen to the word of the LORD! This is what the Sovereign LORD says: Look! I am going to put breath into you and make you live again! I will put flesh and muscles on you and cover you with skin. I will put breath into you, and you will come to life. Then you will know that I am the LORD.'"

So I spoke this message, just as he told me. Suddenly as I spoke, there was a rattling noise all across the valley. The bones of each body came together and attached themselves as complete skeletons. Then as I watched, muscles and flesh formed over the bones. Then skin formed to cover their bodies, but they still had no breath in them.

Then he said to me, "Speak a prophetic message to the winds, son of man. Speak a prophetic message and say, 'This is what the Sovereign LORD says: Come, O breath, from the four winds! Breathe into these dead bodies so they may live again.'"

So I spoke the message as he commanded me, and breath came into their bodies. They all came to life and stood up on their feet—a great army.

Then he said to me, "Son of man, these bones represent the people of Israel. They are saying, 'We have become old, dry bones—all hope is gone. Our nation is finished.' Therefore, prophesy to them and say, 'This is what the Sovereign LORD says: O my people, I will open your graves of exile and cause you to rise again. Then I will bring you back to the land of Israel. When this happens, O my people, you will know that I am the LORD. I will put my Spirit in you, and you will live again and return home to your own *land. Then you will know that I, the LORD, have spoken, and I have done what I said. Yes, the LORD has spoken!"'*

Kelvin made some choices in Tulsa that put him on a trajectory to destruction emotionally, physically and spiritually. He was shot three times on differing occasions, his best friend died while in prison, and even though he was physically out of prison at this time, he was still facing a 20 year sentence for charges he incurred while drug dealing and auto stealing. To say that he did not battle a sense of hopelessness would be a lie, my son was in a battle for his very existence, but he did not have the inner strength to make the right choices, so he did what was easy and he defaulted back to his old friends, his old ways and his old attitudes.

It is one thing to get out jail, it is a whole other thing to get out of the crew you run with, the attitudes you live with and the pain you daily deal with. He was free from a physical jail, at least temporarily, but he was still locked up on the inside. I saw this in him and told him he needed to come back to church, to give Jesus a chance and to let Jesus heal his heart, so he can live again. I did all I could to share the gospel with him in words and in the change of life I had experienced, but despite my best efforts he was unable and unwilling to make those necessary changes.

I remember one day, Kelvin called me and said, "Mom, I think I am going to die!" I had the same sense in my spirit, so when he said this it was a confirmation to what I was hearing, so I told him yet again, son you have to mend your ways, alter your lifestyle, make some radical changes, these are warning signs from God as an act of mercy to save your life. Three months after this conversation, Kelvin stopped selling

> *One thing about the drug life is that it is a web and once you are tangled up in it, it is very difficult to get out of it.*

drugs, but he kept rolling with his same friends. The Bible says that bad company corrupts good character, so I knew that he would not be safe as long as he was hanging out with his old friends, even though he had stopped selling drugs.

One thing about the drug life is that it is a web and once you are tangled up in it, it is very difficult to get out of it. From the addictiveness of the actual substance that is being consumed to the people you are selling to and hanging out with. The whole subculture of drug dealing is very interconnected, so trying to get out of it takes a lot of strength, determination and will power for a variety of reasons. So, when someone says, while why did he not just switch friends, stop smoking, or quit selling, I tell them it is easier said than done. For my son to stop selling drugs was a big step in the right direction, but he still had one foot firmly planted in that lifestyle with those people, so he was not free yet, but little did I know he would not be free from this life while living on earth.

I was living in Kansas at this time but was continually and constantly commuting to Tulsa for multiple reasons. One being the ministry I was interconnected with, the other was a man that I met, Rick, and eventually married. When Rick and I got married, we moved to Kansas. There were more business opportunities there for us than in Tulsa. Kelvin did not like me getting married and he made that very clear to both Rick and I. Rick was not Kelvin's daddy and since I was a single mom for the majority of his life, the idea that his momma was getting married did not sit well with my son. On one hand, I was honored by his protection of me, on the other, I had been single my whole life and longed to be married, so when Rick proposed, there was not much question, for I had heard from God on the subject, and for me, that was the only approval I needed.

Rick and I are now married and living in Kansas. Kelvin still lived in Tulsa, but me being married changed things for Kelvin, because up to this point I was still financially supporting my grown son, who had a proven track record of being irresponsible and now this man, who is my husband, said, it is time to make some financial changes in his life, so he can become a man and support himself and his own family. This alteration did not go well with Kelvin, which added to his animosity toward Rick and his frustration with me. He knew we were for him and not against him, but this drying up of a stream of income affected him, so he engaged even more with his friends that were a bad influence on him. But, I did not know to what level until one night, I had a strong sense in my spirit that I needed to call him, because something was about to go wrong.

I don't know about you, but there are times when I get a sense in my spirit, as a mother, some would call it a mother's intuition, but you just know something is not right. This is the feeling I had, but I did not act upon this feeling,

I just pushed it away, for there was no other reason for me to believe anything would be wrong with my son. I knew in my spirit I should call him, but I never did, and to this day the pain of not making that phone call pricks at me, for that night my son was shot and killed.

Kelvin got a ride with some friends and while in the car he called another friend of his and said, something doesn't feel right, I think these guys are up to something. Kelvin's friend said, get out of the car, just open the door, jump out and run. So, Kelvin took the friends advice and did just that, little did he know the guys in the car, had a gun and took aim and shot him in the back of the head as he was running away from the vehicle. If that was not enough, they went over to his dying body and robbed him of all the possessions he had on his personally and left him for dead.

I got a call at 3:13am on March 28, 2011, I remember the day like it was today. Someone had called 911 and my son was lying in a hospital in Tulsa, OK in a coma. Rick and I immediately got in our car and drove down to Tulsa to be by my son's side. He was in the coma for seven days, before he eventually took his last breath and crossed over on April 5, 2011. On the second day of being in a coma, I heard in the spirit, Kelvin saying, mom let me go. I was praying like a mad woman for my son, I was not going to let him die, this was my boy. Then on the fifth day that he was in the coma, I heard the spirit of the Lord say, "You are washing a corpse, today's a new beginning." On the seventh day of being in the comma, Kelvin died. I washed that boy's body, soul and spirit with my tears in that

No mother should have to bury her child, the pain I experienced is indescribable, if you have never lost a child, I am not sure you can understand the grief I went through and if you have, I hope my story is another level of healing for you.

hospital room. The memories both good and bad flooded my memory. The tears were healing for me, cleansing for him and bottled up for God. No mother should have to bury her child. The pain I experienced is indescribable, if you have never lost a child, I am not sure you can understand the grief I went through and if you have, I hope my story is another level of healing for you. I was not going to let my son die in vain. I knew I had to get his story out for the world to hear, for in his death, I found a new level of life, but it was not before I entered a season of grief that would take me to deep darkness before it brought me into glorious light.

Chapter 4

DARK NIGHT OF THE SOUL

Psalm 42

As the deer longs for streams of water,

so I long for you, O God.

I thirst for God, the living God.

When can I go and stand before him?

Day and night I have only tears for food,

while my enemies continually taunt me,

saying, "Where is this God of yours?"

My heart is breaking

as I remember how it used to be:

I walked among the crowds of worshipers,

leading a great procession to the house of

God, singing for joy and giving thanks

amid the sound of a great celebration!

Why am I discouraged?

Why is my heart so sad?

I will put my hope in God!

I will praise him again—

my Savior and 6 *my God!*

Now I am deeply discouraged,

but I will remember you—even from distant

Mount Hermon, the source of the Jordan,

from the land of Mount Mizar.

I hear the tumult of the raging seas as your

waves and surging tides sweep over me.

But each day the LORD pours his unfailing love

upon me, and through each night I sing his

songs, praying to God who gives me life.

"O God my rock," I cry,

  "Why have you forgotten me?

Why must I wander around in grief,

  oppressed by my enemies?"

Their taunts break my bones.

  They scoff, "Where is this God of yours?"

Why am I discouraged?

  Why is my heart so sad?

I will put my hope in God!

  I will praise him again—

  my Savior and my God!

David in this Psalm shares with such eloquence and poetic prowess what I went through after the death of my, at the time, youngest son. My heart was broken, my eyes were darkened by the grief, my spirit was sobbing with questions as to why God, why. The deep seediness of my grief was beyond what I could put into words, was deeper than emotions could properly convey, so I shut down. I went inside and without cognitive knowledge, I slipped into depression. I could not handle the pain of the loss I just suffered. My heart was broken in ways I did not know possible, but not only was I in pain, my whole family was suffering from this loss of Kelvin, but I was so blinded by my own pain, I could not see how hurt my other family members were.

My oldest son Kevin went to jail four days after his younger brother's death and he spent six months in jail. But Kevin's grief was not situational, it became continual and, in many ways, he still has not healed from the loss of his brother. Actually, he got stuck in the stage of denial, which shut him down emotionally, and to this day, he is locked in a prison of grief and refuses to ask for help.

His family suffers alongside of him. His daughter is living separate from him because of the pain of the loss is so great for him. His wife and the kids are suffering because of his suffering. The cycle of grief is affecting more than just him. It is affecting others around him.

The cycle of grief as noted by psychologists is more complex than can be noted here, but the basic understanding is a 5 stages process as cited by grief.com, which says, these 5 stages of grief are because love never dies.

Stage 1 is denial. According to grief.com this stage helps us survive the loss. It is like when we cut our finger, our first reaction is to grab that finger to stop the bleeding. We do not want to look at the pain, we just want to stop the bleeding, for we are in denial that the cut happened. The same is true with grieving, when we loss someone we love, our first reaction emotionally is denial.

Stage 2 is anger: Anger is a necessary stage in the grieving process, for as people we were not created to supress emotions, but to express them. We are responsive human beings and anger is a response that must be expressed as a process of grieving that will lead to healing. Anger is like a wall of protection for a broken heart. If we do not admit we are angry, we will seek to supress that emotion and one of two things will happen, we will implode (self-harm) or explode. Many outbursts of anger are evidence of a deeply hurt heart. This is why it is imperative that we allow people to express anger, so they can get those emotions out as it pertains to their grieving process.

Stage 3 is bargaining (according to grief.com). "After a loss, bargaining may take the form of a temporary truce. "What if I devote the rest of my life to helping others. Then can I wake up and realize this has all been a bad dream?" We become lost in a maze of "If only..." or "What if..." statements" (grief.com). Seeking to find answers to our questions, being willing to do anything to have that person back is synonymous with this stage of grief and is a necessary stage in the healing process.

Stage 4 is depression. "Empty feelings present themselves, and grief enters our lives on a deeper level, deeper than we ever imagined. This depressive stage feels as though it will last forever. It's important to understand that this depression is not a sign of mental illness. It is the appropriate response to a great loss" (grief.com). Recognizing this is situational depression and allowing people to go through this process is critical to their healing. I know this all too well. This is the phase I went through, and it felt very dark. I did not know if it would ever end, but now looking back I realize it was situational depression, not medicatable depression. Thank God for the process of healing and the varying stages. Truly, the truth is what sets us free (John 8:32).

Stage 5 is grief acceptance. Learning to live with the reality that the person is dead, they will never be coming home again, is a very hard pill to swallow, but a necessary part of the healing process. "We will never like this reality or make it OK, but eventually we accept it. We learn to live with it. It is the new norm with which we must learn to live. We must try to live now in a world where our loved one is missing" (grief.com). This stage can be just as difficult to navigate as the other stages as guilt rises up and says, how can you keep living even though they are dead. I had to come to grips with the reality my son was not going to return to earth, but I was still here and had to keep living. It was not an easy stage to navigate, but it brought a freedom that I needed to live, even though my son had died.

I wish I could tell you that my oldest son Kevin has navigated these stages of grief, but he has not. He in many ways is still bouncing between denial and anger with seeds of depression trying to take root, but the truth is, just as I made it through these stages into healing, I am praying, believing, standing with my oldest son for the same thing. As you look at these stages of grief, I hope you can see where you are in the process of grieving. It does not have to be the loss of a child like I experienced, it could be the loss of a dream, a job, a spouse, a family member, many things are lost in our lives and the same stages of grief must be navigated even though the significance of the loss is measured by the value of that which was lost. Losing a child is much harder to navigate than the loss of a job, but the loss is still painful.

For me, these stages were challenging. My marriage to Rick suffered as I struggled to navigate these stages of grief. I slipped into situational depression for about a year and my marriage took a hit because of it. I felt as though my husband was insensitive to my pain and I even got to the point of considering divorcing him. When you are in intense pain, finding someone to blame, when you are reaching out for help is all part of the process of healing. Rick was not my problem, my pain was, but he was an easy target since he was outside of me and visible, not inside of me and invisible.

In addition to my marriage suffering, our finances and business took a hit, for I was emotionally unable to function. I ended up taking time off as the leader of our business so I could grieve, and my presence being removed was detrimental to the business and our numbers went down which means our revenue took a hit. So, now with our marriage having challenges, my money acting funny and my heart broken, I felt at times like I was going to lose it. I felt out of control, helpless and frustrated that I could not speed this grieving process up. I pressed on through the pain, kept working the stages of grief, kept crying out to

God for help, and eventually, the dark night of my soul gave way to a new hope.

Grief is like a storm, it touches every area of our lives, but I could hear God say, in the midst of the storm, "THIS, TOO, WILL PASS! GRIEVING LASTS FOR THE NIGHT BUT JOY COMES IN THE MORNING!" You know hearing the voice of God in the midst of intense pain is like being given a cool glass of water on a steamy hot summer day. It was refreshing, reviving, rejuvenating, and life-giving. I do not think I would have made it out of the stage of depression if it was not for the Word of God that kept ringing in my soul saying, "THIS,

TOO, WILL PASS! GRIEVING LASTS FOR THE NIGHT BUT JOY COMES IN THE MORNING!"

I remember asking God when my morning was coming. It was still night inside of me, but I knew I heard the voice of God promising me a morning, a breaking of a new day, an awakening of the dawn.

Grieving was robbing my capacity to think clearly, it stole my prayer life and I was mad at God. I tried to stay at a distance from Him, but God wooed me back to Himself with His still small voice. Promising me a new day, a new morning.

Numbers 23:19 says, *"God is not a man, that He should lie, Nor a son of man, that He should repent. Has He said, and will He not do? Or has He spoken, and will He not make it good?"*

When God says something to us, He will do it. We can lean on His promises with all our weight, without fear of being dropped. It was not something I felt, it was something I knew with a certainty, based on the Word of God and the words of God.

What I learned through this dark night of my soul is that pain reflects or better said, exposes your relationship with God. I learned that loss will shut you down; you will feel suffocated. It can cause you to lose your mind when you are grieving. I found it hard to remember the pain, because it was easier to shove it down inside of me than to let it come into the light of God's Word and be healed. Pain exposes your relationship with God, because when you go through pain, you either run to God or run away from Him.

For many people, they may be out of prison, long pass the date of the loss of their first marriage, their child's death or that miscarriage, but even though they believe they are pass it, if they have not dealt with the pain of it, they may be away from it physically, but they are still in bondage to it emotionally.

When we are willing to work through the 5 stages of grief, it will lead to a healing that will set you free physically, emotionally and spiritually.

Remember the 5 stages of grief according to grief.com are:

Stage 1- Denial

Stage 2 – Anger

Stage 3 – Bargaining

Stage 4 – Depression

Stage 5 – Acceptance

Take an honest assessment of where you are in the grieving process if you have suffered a loss. Everyone is in a different stage, but we are all on the same road to recovery. Join us in the journey as we leave the dark night of the soul and embark on the awakening of a new day. The worst is over, and the best is yet to come!

Chapter 5

TIME TO LIVE AGAIN

Psalm 126

When the LORD brought back his exiles to
Jerusalem, it was like a dream!
We were filled with laughter,
     and we sang for joy.
And the other nations said,
     "What amazing things the LORD has done
     for them."
Yes, the LORD has done amazing things for us!
     What joy!
Restore our fortunes, LORD,
     as streams renew the desert.
Those who plant in tears
     will harvest with shouts of joy.

They weep as they go to plant their seed, but they sing as they return with the harvest.

I finally made it to the final stage of grief, I learn to accept the reality that my son was gone and would never return to me in this life on earth. It was a long journey. It was a painful journey, but it was a healing journey not just for me but for others. I have come to realize that our pain when healed becomes the path in which others can walk. Jesus said in John 16:33, "In this world you will have trouble, but take heart, I have overcome the world." Jesus experienced incredible grief while on earth as the people He created rejected Him as their Messiah, but even despite all the grief He suffered, He was able to declare, "...unless a grain of wheat falls to the ground and dies, it remains a single seed. But if it dies, it produces much fruit" (John 12:24).

Jesus' death on the cross and resurrection from the dead, was a path that I have had the distinct privilege of walking as I buried my son, who didn't die on a cross, but just like Jesus died unjustly. So, with the same hope Jesus proclaimed, I say to you, that whatever you have lost, whatever has died in your life, the Lord tells us that while living it only remained a single seed, but now that it is dead, it is about to produce much fruit. My son's death was not in vain, for it produced in me a new hope, a new dream, a new vision of what God wanted to do in the lives of others who have suffered loss and of my own life.

When I was grieving I could not see the "light at the end of the tunnel," when I was inside the belly of the whale. It was dark, damp and depressing, but now that God has spit me back out on shore, has healed my heart and set me free. I have a vision for the future. I have a hope for my region and I have a ministry that is touching many. Would you follow me for just one more stage in my process of healing as I share with you what God gave me as part of my healing?

God continued to say to me over and over again, "I'm going to restore you. By my stripes you are healed!" and I can stand here and testify to this reality, that I had no other way out, but God. I was living in the belly of that whale, but God; I was lingering in depression, but God; I was without hope, but God; I was lost in my own thoughts, but God! My process had to come to a place of healing, for God to give to me what He had prepared for me and it started with me remembering who I was. I was a worshipper. I was a psalmist. I was a prophetess. I was an intercessor. I was a gap stander and God reminded me of who I was, but not only that, He opened up a door for who I was to meet who I was going to become.

Today, my husband and I own several businesses. One is a group home for children with disabilities. There are only boys in this home. We sow seeds of love and the Word of God inside of these boys, so that they can take

> *I have seen many people delivered and healed from grief and addictions. The same giant that tried to keep me down.*

the Journey that God has chosen for them. I believe what the devil meant for bad, God will turn it around for the good. I am now doing Omani outreaches in many different states -- prayer summit they are called Sound Summits. I have seen many people delivered and healed from grief and addictions, which was the same giant that tried to keep me down.

God has a plan! My marriage is awesome, and we are doing the will of the Lord. My grandchildren are growing, and my children are working out their soul's salvation with trembling in fear. I thank God for what He's done for me and my family. Healing is real: I am that testimony.

Out of the death of my son Kelvin, came the ministry I am President and founder of, "Meet Me At The Wall" (www.meetmeatthewall.org). Meet Me At The Wall is a region taking, prayer making, prophecy speaking ministry that has been called to heal the people, so we can heal the land. We have a prayer call every Saturday morning at 6am cst, in which intercessors from New York to California gather to pray for our nation, our people and our regions. God has been faithful to speak prophetically through this small band of believers that come together every Saturday and we are shifting atmospheres with our prayers. I have learned not only who I am, who I am called to be, but also the authority I have. Pain has a way of making you stronger, so when opposition arises, I am not moved, for the greatest gift was taken from me and God allowed me to rise from the ashes, so there is nothing anyone can say to me that can get me to get off the wall.

Meet Me At The Wall was birthed in May 2012, just over a month after the first anniversary of my son's death. My mentor, mother and friend Prophetess Brenda Todd of Gap Standers International was the midwife for the birthing of this new ministry. Without her advice, counsel, correction and help with direction, this ministry would not be what it is today. She not only helped birth it, she helped me lay a solid foundation on the Word of God, so this wall would be strong, stable and able to withstand the attacks that would come against it. I am forever grateful to this woman of God for all she has done for me and been to me in my life.

Before the wall was birthed, God told me, I have a baby on the inside of me that is going to heal nations, regions and lands. This has happened on a region level, and it is in the process of being on a national and international level, for God said it, and He always does what He says He's going to do.

Isaiah 55:10-13

"The rain and snow come down from the

    heavens and stay on the ground to water

    the earth.

They cause the grain to grow,

   producing seed for the farmer

   and bread for the hungry.

It is the same with my word.

   I send it out, and it always produces fruit.

It will accomplish all I want it to,

   and it will prosper everywhere I send it.

You will live in joy and peace.

The mountains and hills will burst into song,

and the trees of the field will clap their hands!

Where once there were thorns, cypress trees

will grow.

Where nettles grew, myrtles will sprout up.

These events will bring great honor to

the LORD's name; they will be an

everlasting sign of his power and love."

From the barrenness and decrease I was experiencing during the depression stage of my healing to the acceptance of my son's death, I found expansion happening all around me. My marriage was increasing in communication, intimacy and companionship. My business was back on track and on a trajectory to restore the losses I incurred financially. The ministry was not only doing the weekly prayer line, it started doing what we called Sound Summits yearly, drawing people from all over the nation as I had received a mandate from God to rebuild the walls in prayer, similar what Nehemiah was called to do in the Bible after his name. Everything was expanding all around me and the joy of the Lord was my strength for in many ways, I did not feel equipped for all the prosperity and expansion I was experiencing, but God!

The healing I was experiencing through God's power was changing my life as well as the lives of many people around me.

God gave me the idea for this ministry when Kelvin was 17 years old, but it took eight years and a lot of pain in order for this ministry to be birthed, but I can say with confidence now, I would not want to go through that again, but I know Romans 8:27-29 is true from experience, *"And He who searches our hearts knows the mind of the Spirit, because the Spirit intercedes for the saints according to the will of God.* And we know that God works all things together for the good of those who love Him, who are called according to His purpose. For those God foreknew, He also *predestined to be conformed to the image of His Son"*.

Here are some of the things people who have been a part of The Wall Ministry have said about their experience.

Prophetess Maureena and Rick Summers, establishers of The Wall Association, are certainly jewels of God's kingdom. Prophetess Summers and I path divinely crossed some eight or nine years ago, and my life and the lives of my children have been forever changed. Their educational facility has been one of the driving forces in educating my three children and numerous others, assisting the next generation with flourishing into their God ordained destiny.

By the example of Prophetess summers, myself and many others have learned the importance and transforming power of prayer, supplication and worship to almighty God. With this knowledge and the wisdom to apply it, I now pastor a local ministry.

Thank you, Prophetess Maureena and Rick Summers for your commitment and dedication to educate children, empower God's people and to build God's kingdom one soul at a time.

Pastor Carlashoun Bagby

Ark of Triumph Ministries

Kansas City, MO

Since becoming part of the Wall Ministry, I now pray with a more God center purpose, and my spiritual walk with God is becoming stronger each and every day. Thank you Prophetess Maureena for teaching me about the about the prophetic, dream interpretation, and most of all seeing the miraculous move of God in the Sound Summits; when we were praying last year at Battery Park in New York City, and seeing the spirit move after praying, decreeing and declaring, and planting the Vavs, WOW IT'S BEEN AWESOME! I look forward to more and more of God's hand moving the Nations of the world, my family and in my life in this turnaround season of recovery.

Xenia Pena

New York, USA

In 2014, while attending Refreshing Waters Worship Center in Kansas City, MO, I had the privilege of meeting Prophetess Maureena Summers at a prayer meeting. Little did I know that this meeting would turn into a ministry partnership. Now 4 years later, we have redug wells together all over the United States, we have hosted Sound Summit's together in various states, we have spent countless hours in prayer together, we have fellowshipped together, ate meals together, joined our families together and we have seen God bring healing to both of our lives, yes together. I am honored to know Prophetess Maureena Summers and have been blessed beyond definition by the ministry called The Wall. My heart is with this woman on God, my prayers are for her success and my experiences with her will never be forgotten. But I must say, her words are what stick with me more than anything, for she is a distributor of hope, for she continues to make the word of God her standard, the prophecy of God her steering wheel and the statement of God her light, when she declares at the end of every Saturday morning prayer call, the best is yet to come! We haven't seen *anything yet my friend, truly the best is yet to come.*

Lisa Great, President, Apostolic Resource Center

Kansas City, MO

Hearing how other people view what God has done in this ministry is truly the fuel that keeps me going when the days are long, the mornings are early and at times the offerings are lean. I have learned to love more; give more; and never forget my first love, who is Jesus. These things have accelerated my healing and continue to do so.

I believe I was, I am a Jonah, but I'm now in Nineveh and people are being healed. God alone is the healer and He loves to heal.

Psalm 103

Let all that I am praise the LORD; with my

whole heart, I will praise his holy name.

Let all that I am praise the LORD;

may I never forget the good things he does

for me.

He forgives all my sins

and heals all my diseases.

He redeems me from death

and crowns me with love and tender

mercies.

He fills my life with good things.

My youth is renewed like the eagle's!

The LORD gives righteousness

and justice to all who are treated unfairly.

He revealed his character to Moses

and his deeds to the people of Israel.

The LORD is compassionate and merciful,

slow to get angry and filled with unfailing

love.

He will not constantly accuse us,

nor remain angry forever.

He does not punish us for all our sins;

he does not deal harshly with us, as we

deserve.

For his unfailing love toward those who fear

him is as great as the height of the heavens

above the earth.

He has removed our sins as far from us

as the east is from the west.

The LORD is like a father to his children,

  tender and compassionate to those who fear

  him.

For he knows how weak we are;

  he remembers we are only dust.

Our days on earth are like grass;

  like wildflowers, we bloom and die.

The wind blows, and we are gone—

  as though we had never been here.

But the love of the LORD remains forever

  with those who fear him.

His salvation extends to the children's children

  of those who are faithful to his covenant,

  of those who obey his commandments!

The LORD has made the heavens his throne;

from there he rules over everything.

Praise the LORD, you angels,

you mighty ones who carry out his plans,

listening for each of his commands.

Yes, praise the LORD, you armies of angels

who serve him and do his will!

Praise the LORD, everything he has created,

everything in all his kingdom.

Let all that I am praise the LORD.

We will not get off the wall until we heal the people, heal the land. We cannot heal people, God alone can do that. But He has chosen to use us and to use you as vessels of healing. If you want to join us on the wall, we would be honored to have you as a ministry partner and here are some of the ways you can do just that.

1. You can join us Saturday mornings at 6am cst as we intercede for our nation, our regions and our world. The number to call is: 641.715.3200, access code 485127.

2. You can become a financial partner by going to www.meetmeatthewall.org and clicking the donate button.

3. You can sign up to be on our email list, which will provide you with information about our Sound Summit's, along with other places we will be ministering around the nation.

4. You can choose to pray for us, whether you let us know you are doing it or not, for we know this ministry is fueled by the power of God and prayer.

No matter how you decide to partner with us, we want you to know we exist for your healing and count it a privilege to serve the body of Christ in this way. Little did I know that this ministry would be birthed out of the ashes of a broken heart like mine, but what I do know is that I am forever grateful to the one who called me out of darkness and into His marvelous light, and if He did it for me, I want you to know He can do it for you. You are not alone, we are in this with you!

Thank you for making the time to read this book, I hope it was an encouragement to you on your journey of healing or that it becomes a resource for you as you walk with someone else that is in the process of navigating the stages of grief for a loss they may have suffered. My desire in writing this was to be a blessing to those who may be struggling with loss on a variety of levels and to be a sign on the dark road of recovery, encouraging you to keep going, for His word is a lamp unto your feet and a light unto your path, just as it was for me. You are not alone, we are standing on the wall, praying for you. Remember, Nineveh is just around the corner.

Jonah 3

Then

the LORD spoke to

Jonah a second

time: "Get up and

go to the great

city of Nineveh,

and deliver the

message I have

given you."

This time Jonah

obeyed

the LORD's

command and

went to Nineveh,

a city so large

that it took three
days to see it all.
On the day Jonah
entered the city,
he shouted to the
crowds: "Forty
days from now
Nineveh will be

destroyed!" The
people of Nineveh
believed God's
message, and
from the greatest
to the least, they
declared a fast
and put on

burlap to show
their sorrow.

When the king of
Nineveh heard
what Jonah was
saying, he
stepped down
from his throne

and took off his
royal robes. He
dressed himself
in burlap and sat
on a heap of
ashes. Then the
king and his
nobles sent this

decree

throughout the

city:

"No one, not even

the animals from

your herds and

flocks, may eat or

drink anything at

all. People and animals alike must wear garments of mourning, and everyone must pray earnestly to God. They must turn from their evil ways and stop all their violence. Who can tell? Perhaps even yet God will change his mind and hold back his *fierce anger from*

destroying us."

When God saw

what they had

done and how

they had put a

stop to their evil

ways, he changed

his mind and did not carry out the destruction he had threatened.

God bless you and remember THE BEST IS YET TO COME!

Made in the USA
Lexington, KY
25 October 2019